P9-ECP-178

# FOSSILS

Written by JOHN BURTON

Illustrated by JOHN BARBER

BISON
(BISON ANTIQUUS)

MASTODON
(MAMMUT AMERICANUS)

Publishers · GROSSET & DUNLAP · New York
A FILMWAYS COMPANY

SCOLOSAURUS

# INTRODUCTION

Fossils, the remains of extinct animals and plants, are much more in evidence than most people realize. For instance, coal is the remains of plants that lived in swampy forests millions of years ago. Limestone, often used as building stone, is the remains of extinct sea creatures. Amber, used for making jewelry, is the fossilized remains of resin from pine trees. Chalk, oil, and many other substances are fossil remains of extinct plants and animals from long ago.

Occasionally, more spectacular fossils are found — dinosaurs in North America, frozen mammoths in Siberia, cave bears in the Alps, and so forth. But *anyone* can find fossils. By looking carefully in chalk, limestone, or coal, it is always possible to find a really beautiful fossil.

Library of Congress Catalog Card Number: 75-4015
ISBN: 0-448-05076-5 (Wonder Book Edition)
ISBN: 0-448-04074-3 (Trade Edition)
ISBN: 0-448-03870-6 (Library Edition)
Published in the United States by
Grosset & Dunlap, Inc., New York, N.Y.

FIRST PRINTING 1976

Originally published in Great Britain
by Transworld Publishers Ltd.
Transworld Edition Published 1974.
Copyright © 1974 Transworld Publishers Ltd.
All Rights Reserved.
Printed in the United States of America.

# CONTENTS

DIRE WOLVES

# Fossils — A History of the Past

**What are fossils?** Fossils are the remains of animals and plants that have been preserved in rocks. There are many ways this can happen: after an animal dies, its skeleton may be preserved without changing much; over many years the bones may be replaced with rock; or the animal may dissolve away and the space it leaves becomes filled with mud or sand, which slowly hardens into rock.

The best fossils are usually formed when a dead animal or plant falls into very fine mud and is quickly covered over. For this reason the animals and plants living in swamps and river estu-aries are often well preserved, as rivers are often full of fine mud and sand known as "silt." The word "fossil" comes from a Latin word that means to dig up. Originally, a fossil was anything dug up out of the ground, but now we use the word only for the remains of once-living things. By studying the types of fossils from long ago, scientists can reconstruct the world as it was in the past. Some kinds of plants and animals grow in warm climates, others in forests, and so on. If such fossils are found, it is possible to deduce the climate and also what the world looked like.

VULTURE

SMILODON

WOOLLY RHINOCEROS

A rhinoceros trapped in a swamp is easy prey for the fierce Smilodon. It has also attracted wolves and vultures.

When fossils are found as a complete set of "associated" bones (where the bones are all together in such a way that it is obvious that they all came from one animal), it is often possible to put the skeleton together and start reconstructing right away. More frequently, however, the bones are crushed and broken, and usually only part of a skeleton is found. First, the bones must be repaired and restored, and then a concept of the complete skeleton may be possible. Placing the bits together often takes many months of careful work in a laboratory. Sometimes the evidence from several bits of skeletons is combined

**How are reconstructions of fossils made?**

to make a single model of a complete skeleton.

The next stage is to compare the bones with other fossils, and also with those of animals still living. Each of the bones is then examined very carefully for the small lumps and bumps that indicate where the muscles were attached. These small lumps and bumps may even suggest approximately how big and powerful the muscles were. Usually the scientist and an artist work together. The scientist informs the artist as to how the animal should appear and the artist sketches or models it. The scientist then compares the sketch or model with the fossil bones and tells the artist of any alterations.

5

When a model is being made, the artist often makes up a framework based on the skeleton, and then builds up the muscles onto it, finally clothing the whole animal in a "skin." The finished details of color, length of fur, and so on, are usually mostly guesswork. Normally, the color is determined by comparing the fossil with a similar living animal that lives in the same sort of habitat. But this can often be misleading — after all, the bones of a horse and a zebra look similar, and they both live in open grasslands — yet they appear quite different.

**How are models of fossils made?**

An artist forming model of a woolly mammoth.

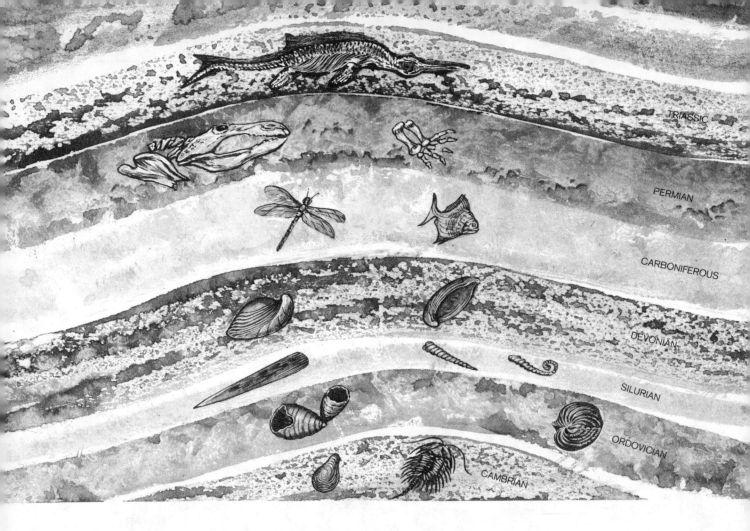

A diagram of Earth's strata, showing the kind of fossils found in each layer.

Paleontologists (scientists studying fossils) using very powerful microscopes have found the fossilized remains of bacteria and other simple forms of life in rocks about 3 billion years old. The rocks in which certain fossils are found are often similar, and they also contain the same kind of fossils in different parts of the world. Over millions of years the rocks formed on top of one another. The layers are known as *strata*. These strata have been given names to make them easier to remember. The time it took them to build up varies. For instance,

**When did the first fossils live?**

the table on pages 8 and 9 shows that the Pleistocene Period lasted only about 2½ million years, but the Permian lasted about 55 million years.

During the Cambrian Period, which began over 570 million years ago, the first really recognizable plants and animals began to develop. Fossils of many different animals have been found, but they are all invertebrates—that is, animals without backbones. The animals with backbones (known as *vertebrates*), such as fish, amphibians, reptiles, birds, and mammals, did not evolve on this planet until many millions of years later.

7

## A TIME SCALE OF EARTH HISTORY

| Eras | | Periods and Epochs | When They Began | Changes in Lands, Seas, and Living Things |
|---|---|---|---|---|
| **CENOZOIC** Era of Mammals | Quaternary Period | Recent Epoch (Holocene) | 8,000 to about 10,000 years ago | Great glaciers melted for the last time; climates grew warm. Many large land mammals died out near the end of the period. |
| | | Pleistocene Epoch, also called the Great Ice Age | 2.5 to 3 million years ago | Glaciers repeatedly spread over much of Europe, Asia, and North America. Climates and seas were cold when glaciers spread, but warm during interglacial times. Mammals grew large and varied; man evolved. |
| | Tertiary Period | Pliocene Epoch | 13 million years ago | High mountains, including the Rockies, formed as this period began. The Andes, Alps, Cascades, and Himalayas rose in later epochs. Seas seldom covered much of the continents. Mammals became common and varied on land; sharks and bony fish were plentiful. Modern types of corals, clams, snails, etc., became dominant in seas; ammonites and belemnites died out, but squids and octopuses became common. Land plants became more and more like those of the present day. Apelike ancestors of man evolved. |
| | | Miocene Epoch | 25 million years ago | |
| | | Oligocene Epoch | 40 million years ago | |
| | | Eocene Epoch | 55 million years ago | |
| | | Paleocene Epoch | 65 million years ago | |
| **MESOZOIC** Era of Reptiles | | Cretaceous Period | 136 million years ago | Lands generally were low, climates were mild, and bird-hipped dinosaurs were abundant and varied. Seas spread widely; ammonites, belemnites, and relatives of oysters were common, as were marine reptiles. |
| | | Jurassic Period | 180 million years ago | Lands were low; seas covered much of Europe; there were deserts, volcanoes, and swampy forests in western North America. Marine reptiles were common near the end of the period. Dinosaurs became very large and spread around the world. Birds evolved. |
| | | Triassic Period | 230 million years ago | Seas covered much of Europe; ammonites became common. Ichthyosaurs and early plesiosaurs evolved, as did other reptilian groups and mammals. Lizard-hipped dinosaurs became common, but most of them were small. |

| | Period | Time | Description |
|---|---|---|---|
| **PALEOZOIC** Era of Ancient Life | Permian Period | 280 million years ago | Coal swamps were much reduced; mountains formed in eastern North America; glaciers spread in South Africa. Large amphibians and reptiles lived in swampy lowlands; sharklike fish and early ammonoids were common. |
| | Carboniferous Period | 345 million years ago | Coal was deposited in great swamps; seas spread but did not last long; mountain-building continued in the East and in Europe. Amphibians and reptiles became large and common. Seas covered much of North America, especially during the early part of this period. |
| | Devonian Period | 400 million years ago | Most of North America was low and flat; seas spread widely, though mountains began to rise and forests grew on low deltas. In the Old Red basins of Europe, fish evolved into amphibians as they tried to remain in water. |
| | Silurian Period | 440 million years ago | Europe remained mountainous, but most of North America was low and much of it was under salt water. Marine life was abundant; jawless "fish" continued to evolve; sea scorpions were common in brackish waters. |
| | Ordovician Period | 500 million years ago | Shifting seas covered more than half of North America, but mountains formed in the East and in Europe. Most corals remained small, but brachiopods and trilobites became common, and straight cephalopods grew very large. |
| | Cambrian Period | 570 to 620 million years ago | Most of North America was low, after mountain-building in the Great Lakes region at the end of Precambrian times. Marine animals, especially brachiopods and trilobites, became common fossils, but many other groups existed. |
| | **PRECAMBRIAN ERAS** (Variously divided on the different continents) | Probably more than 4.6 billion years ago | Many changes in lands and seas; mountain-building in various parts of the world; great volcanic eruptions; formations of important ore deposits; relatively few fossils. |

TRILOBITE

TRILOBITE

Cambrian life

The period before the Cambrian is

**When was Earth formed?**

known as the Precambrian and only a few fossils are evident from these times — only simple bacteria and algae (like the green slime in ponds). Some of these are about 3 billion years old! The Precambrian stretches back to the time when the earth formed — about 4.6 billion years ago.

During the Cambrian Period mollusks (related to slugs and snails) and sea worms were common, and many have been preserved as fossils. Another animal that was common for millions of years, and was first seen during the Cambrian Period, was the *trilobite*. They no longer exist now, but nearly all museum collections of fossils have excellent specimens of trilobites.

The periods did not suddenly end,

**What came after the Cambrian period?**

but conditions gradually changed, taking thousands, or even millions, of years. The Ordovician Period, which followed the Cambrian, began approximately 500 million years ago and lasted for about 60 million years. The seas of the Ordovician Period were full of life — and some of the animals were similar to those still alive today. There were lots of echinoderms. Echinoderms are animals like starfish, sea urchins and brittle stars. (The name "echinoderm" comes from the Greek words *ekhinos* and *derm,* meaning "hedgehog" and "skin" — many of them, such as sea urchins, have prickly skins.) There were also lots of different mollusks and corals, as well as trilobites. But there were still no animals on dry land.

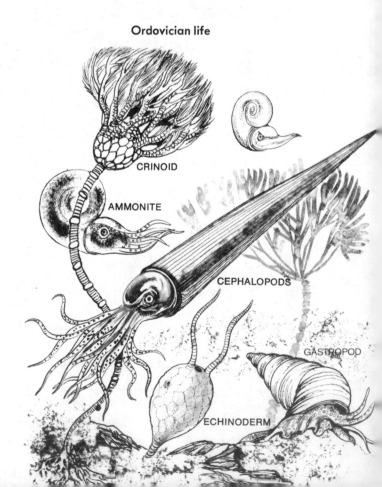

Ordovician life

CRINOID

AMMONITE

CEPHALOPODS

GASTROPOD

ECHINODERM

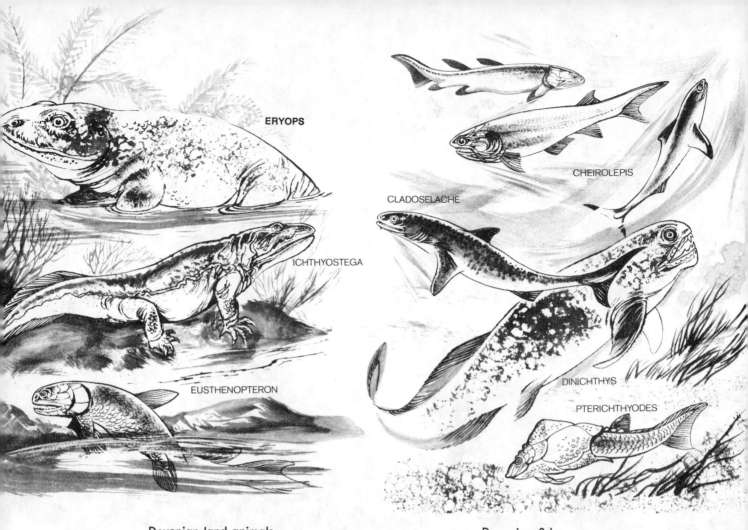

ERYOPS

ICHTHYOSTEGA

EUSTHENOPTERON

CHEIROLEPIS

CLADOSELACHE

DINICHTHYS

PTERICHTHYODES

Devonian land animals

Devonian fishes

Following the Ordovician Period came the Silurian, which started about 440 million years ago and lasted some 40 million years. During this period there were lots of shallow coral seas. They must have been very colorful and full of life.

Land animals probably evolved when the ponds and pools in which they lived kept drying out. Those that managed to survive eventually bred, and gradually land animals breathing air evolved.

**When did land animals evolve?**

The first fossil land animals were like scorpions and millipedes, and they have been found in rocks formed during the Silurian Period. During the Devonian Period, which followed and lasted about 55 million years, even more land animals evolved, including woodlice, spiders, and insects (though not flying insects). The Devonian Period is often called the "Age of Fishes." Many beautifully preserved fossils have been found, and they show that fish evolved into many different shapes and sizes during the Devonian Period. By the end of the Devonian Period amphibians were also around — the first land vertebrates — though they had to return to water in order to breed, just as some insects, such as dragonflies,

Life in Carboniferous times

still do. Amphibians are creatures like frogs, toads, and newts. The name comes from the Greek *amphi* and *bios,* which mean "both kinds" and "life," because these animals live both in water and on land. The period that followed the Devonian was the Carboniferous, which started about 345 million years ago. The Carboniferous was the time when the fossil we know as coal was formed. Coal is the fossilized remains of trees and plants that grew in the swampy forests of the Carboniferous Period — giant ferns and other plants.

If you look at coal carefully, you can often see impressions of plants. Also living in the forests were giant amphibians — salamanderlike animals up to 10 feet long. They probably fed on other amphibians as well as fish. The first reptiles also lived during this period, and insects flew among the trees. The largest insect ever known was a fossil dragonfly, which lived in Carboniferous forests. It had a wingspan of about 3 feet — its remains were found in France.

PETROLACOSAURUS

During the Permian Period, which followed the Carboniferous and started about 280 million years ago, many more different reptiles were found, and often they lived in very dry desert areas. None of the reptiles was very big — the largest was less than 10 feet long. Although it is difficult to know exactly when mammals evolved, we do know that during the Permian some of the reptiles were similar to mammals. From just the fossilized bones, it is always difficult to decide when the first mammals appeared.

**When were mammals first found?**

Life in Permian times

VARANOSAURUS

DIADECTES

DIPLOCAULUS

CACOPS

EDAPHOSAURUS

The dinosaurs included some of the largest animals that have ever existed.

DIMETRODON

DUCK-BILLED DINOSAURS

BRACHIOSAURUS

DIPLODOCUS

**When did the disonaurs live?** The dinosaurs first walked the earth during the Triassic Period, which started 225 million years ago and lasted about 35 million years until the Jurassic Period, which started about 190 million years ago. The Jurassic not only saw the first birds, but also the beginning of the "Age of Reptiles." A wide variety of giant dinosaurs, ichthyosaurs, and pterodactyls had evolved, and they continued to live until they became extinct near the end of the Cretaceous Period, which ended some 65 million years ago. Many famous dinosaur remains come from rocks formed during the Jurassic and Cretaceous Periods.

**When did dinosaurs die out?** By the end of the Cretaceous Period, dinosaurs were extinct. But they did not suddenly die out, as many believe. Over several thousands or even millions of years they slowly disappeared, one by one. Millions of years later, it seems to us as though they became extinct very quickly. No one really knows why the dinosaurs became extinct. There are lots of suggestions; probably changes in the weather, which would alter the plants on which some of them fed, were important. But the dinosaurs did not suddenly go — and they walked the earth for millions of years longer than people have.

The Cretaceous period. Two dinosaurs fight over the carcass of a Stegosaurus.

TYRANOSAURUS

TRICERATOPS

Life in Eocene times

The Paleocene and Eocene, the earliest epochs of the Tertiary Period in the Cenozoic Era, followed the Cretaceous Period. It started about 65 million years ago and lasted 25 million years. During this time mammals (animals that have live babies that nurse on milk) developed into many different kinds. Fossil ancestors of most of the main groups of living mammals can be found in the strata of the Eocene: there are hoofed animals (ungulates), flesh-eaters (carnivores), pouched animals (marsupials), primitive whales (zeuglodonts) and even fossil primates — the ancestors of man.

16

During the Oligocene Epoch, which

**When did modern animals evolve?** lasted about 14 million years and started about 40 million years ago, many fossil mammals and other animals were like modern ones. In fact, many are believed to be direct ancestors of modern animals. During the Miocene Epoch that followed (about 26 million years ago), most of the animals in the world were very similar to the modern types.

Some of the animals of the Oligocene Epoch

Some of the animals of the Miocene Epoch

MESOHIPPUS

INDRICOTHERIUM

ARSINOITHERIUM

OLIGOCENE LANDSCAPE

GOMPHOTHERIUM

PALEOMERYX

TETRALOPHODON

MIOCENE LANDSCAPE

MAMMOTH

MODERN HORSE

MASTODON ANANCUS

PLIOHIPPUS

GOMPHOTHERIUM

HIPPARION

PALAEOMASTODON

MERYCHIPPUS

PHIOMIA

ANCHITHERIUM

MESOHIPPUS

Some of the
ancestors of the
elephant family.

MOERITHERIUM

Some of the
ancestors of the
horse family.

EOHIPPUS

The most recent epoch is known as the Holocene, but scientists are still not certain as to whether or not we are still living in the Pleistocene Epoch. The Pleistocene is often called the Ice Age; but the Ice Age was not continuous — sometimes ice spread out from the poles and came as far as New England, but at other times the weather became quite mild, and the countryside was more like that found in East Africa today, with large animals roaming in abundance.

**Which period do we live in?**

During the Pleistocene Epoch these animals roamed the ground of many of today's cities.

Coal is the fossil remains of swampy forests. Fossils of plants (and even animals) are easy to find in coal.

# Some "Special" Fossils

If you visit a natural history museum,

**What are the most valuable fossils in the world?**

you may walk past the most valuable fossils without even noticing them. The most valuable fossils are oil and coal. They are so valuable that without them modern civilization would stop almost at once. Coal is made from plant remains about 350 million years old, and oil from small forms of life in the sea. At that time much of the earth's surface was covered by luxuriant swamps; the rotting

vegetation that was later covered and trapped underground was transformed into oil and coal. Modern life depends on oil and coal for many things, but some scientists think that we are burning oil and coal so fast that it will soon be used up. It is strange to think that the grandchildren and even the children of the readers of this book will probably see gasoline-fueled cars only in museums. This is because gasoline, like so many other things, is made from natural oil, the substance which was once fossil plants.

Sometimes oil seeps to the surface of the earth to form tar pits. These sticky tar pits become death traps for any animals that walk too close to them. It is in tar pits that some of the best-preserved fossils have been found.

**What animals have been found in tar pits?**

In the famous tar pit at Rancho la Brea in California scientists have found thousands of horses, elephantlike animals, many birds, and other animals that were probably attracted by pools of water on top of the tar. The larger meat-eating animals saw these animals struggling, but when they tried to get at them, they too became trapped. This is how animals like Smilodons (saber-toothed cats) and vultures became caught.

The tar pits at Rancho la Brea trapped many animals. Meat-eating animals, like this saber-toothed cat, were attracted by them. They were also trapped by the tar.

Frozen mammoths have been found in Siberia.

The best-preserved fossils are undoubtedly the frozen mammoths found in Siberia. These have been known for many hundreds of years. Natives living there once believed the mammoth was some sort of giant mole that died as soon as it saw daylight! They fed the meat from the mammoths to their dogs, and collected the ivory from the tusks and traded with it. Until very recently the ivory from mammoths was a very important source of the world's ivory — many works of art in China were made from it.

**Which were the best-preserved fossils ever found?**

One of the best-preserved mammoths was found in 1799, when one was found frozen in a block of ice by a Tungus (an inhabitant of Siberia). Nearly four years after the discovery, the head and tusks began to thaw out of the ice, and the Tungus took a Russian ivory trader to see the mammoth. The trader had never seen a mammoth so well preserved, and so he made some quick drawings and sent them to the Academy in St. Petersburg (now called Leningrad). One of the scientists who saw the drawing was an Englishman named Henry Adams. He organized an expedition to find the mammoth in 1806 and bring back what remained of

22

it. He was lucky and managed to get most of the skin, one ear, and nearly all of the skeleton. Unfortunately, while the thick woolly hide was being taken back to St. Petersburg, most of the hair rubbed off. But Henry Adams pointed out that the fact that mammoths were covered with thick hair meant that they could have lived in the cold North. Until then it had been assumed that the North Pole had moved and that the "elephants" had died when it became cold.

Woolly rhinos have also been found preserved in blocks of ice, but the best specimens of woolly rhinoceroses were two young ones found together with a mammoth calf in Poland. They had been "pickled" by accidentally falling into an oil pit and were then preserved in the paraffin-like oil.

Above — a wasp preserved in a piece of amber.

Bottom — wasps and other insects are often trapped in the sticky resin on pine trees.

**What is amber?** Amber is the fossilized remains of the resin produced by pine trees. In some parts of the world, pine trees are still "tapped" for resin to produce turpentine. The resin is collected in much the same way as rubber is collected — a small cut is made in the side of the tree and a cup hung beneath it to collect the liquid as it oozes out. When a pine tree is damaged or a branch has broken off, you can sometimes see the resin oozing out; if you look closely, you will also often see insects stuck to the resin. More resin may then gradually cover the insect, encasing it in a tomb of resin. This very same thing happened millions of years ago, and amber is the fossil remains of ancient resin, which in the course of time has hardened and become a beautiful clear orange-yellow color. Occasionally, amber is found with insects perfectly preserved within it.

One of the areas of the world that is richest in amber is the Baltic Sea region of the U.S.S.R. For centuries the local inhabitants have collected amber, and nowadays all the amber is owned by the state. In the Middle Ages the "amber route" was a trade route from the Baltic to Constantinople (now known as Istanbul), where the valuable amber was carved into rosaries, necklaces, and other jewelry.

23

Other animals, like spiders and even

**Have other animals been found in amber?** small lizards, have occasionally been found encased in amber. These fossils are particularly interesting, since animals as small and fragile as insects and spiders are seldom preserved. Not only have the whole bodies of small animals been found, but also odd feathers from small birds, and hair from mammals. Seeds and pollen are also found from time to time. Ever since ancient times, collectors have looked for amber containing insects and other animals. In Europe, during the Renaissance period, forgeries were made to fool the enthusiastic and ignorant collectors who would pay high prices for such things. The forger would hollow out the amber and place in it a fish, lizard, or perhaps a frog or a bird, pour linseed oil into the cavity, and carefully plug the opening with another piece of amber.

Among the largest of the dinosaurs is

**What are the largest fossils?** *Apatosaurus (Brontosaurus)*. The fossil remains of this huge animal have been so well preserved that a complete skeleton has been reconstructed in the American Museum of Natural History. In life it was about 65 feet long, and it is estimated that it weighed about 50,000 pounds. But the head and brain were minute in comparison with its body size.

The best specimens have been found in the Jurassic strata of Wyoming, where many dinosaurs have been found. Another well-known giant dinosaur,

*Diplodocus,* though not as bulky as *Apatosaurus,* was longer. It grew to about 97 feet, but this included a very long, slender tail. Philanthropist Andrew Carnegie paid for the excavation of several of these dinosaurs, so a scientist named it after him — *Diplodocus carnegii.* He also paid to have a life-

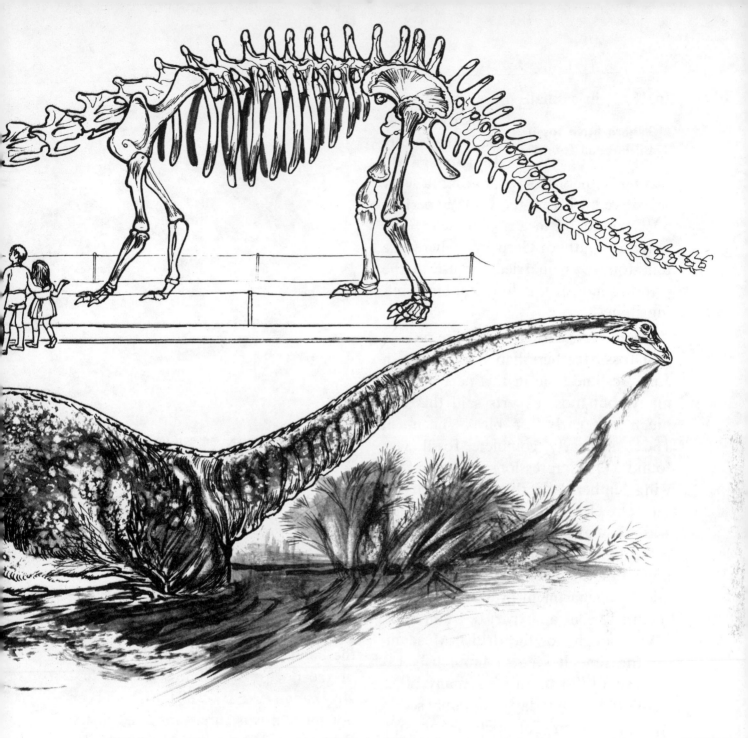

Diplodocus was one of the largest land animals. Millions of years ago it lived in swampy lakes.

sized restoration of the skeleton made, and replicas of it were sent to several other museums. They are on public display in Paris, London, Berlin, and Vienna.

Another giant was *Brachiosaurus,* which was over 80 feet long, over 40 feet high at its head, and weighed 80 tons. Like the two previous species, it probably spent much of its life in swamps and lakes, where it would be safer from its enemies, and the water would help support its vast weight. It probably fed mainly on aquatic vegetation, which it would be able to reach under water with its long neck.

25

In 1861, in a small village in Bavaria,

**Where have fossil birds been found?**
a discovery was made that really demonstrated Darwin's theory of evolution: a very primitive bird from the Jurassic period.

It was found in a quarry near Solnhofen in southern Germany, where fine limestone was quarried for use in the printing industry as lithographic printing stones.

Some years earlier there were rumors that fossil feathers had been found in Jurassic limestone in this part of Germany, but most experts said this was much too early for birds. Then, in 1861, a nearly complete fossil was found. The impressions made by the wing feathers and the feathers on the tail were clearly visible—only the head was missing. The fossil was acquired by a local doctor, who realized its value; and after the Director of the Natural History Department of the British Museum had sent an expert to examine it, it was bought for the British Museum. At the time it seemed fabulously expensive (£700 for it, and many other fossils), though today it probably seems quite a bargain for such an unusual specimen.

Controversy raged over *Archaeopteryx*,

**Was another Archaeopteryx ever found?**
as the fossil bird was called, but gradually experts began to believe that it was indeed a very ancient bird. Anyone who had any doubts about this first specimen thought twice when in 1877 a second *Archaeopteryx* was discovered in

26

ARCHAEOPTERYX

(Above) Archaeopteryx, the earliest known bird, is much more like a reptile than modern birds.

(Right) Some flying reptiles. All flying reptiles are now extinct.

a quarry fairly close to Solnhofen. This specimen was even better preserved than the first — even the head was well preserved. Remarkably, it came into the hands of Ernst Haberlein, the son of the doctor who had sold the first *Archaeopteryx*. By 1881, it had been bought and was safely installed in the Berlin Natural Science Museum. This time German scientists were determined that it should not leave the country (although now it is in East Germany and more difficult to see than the English specimen). Fossils continue to be found in the Bavarian quarries, but it was not until 1956 that another fossil bird was found. This time the specimen was so badly preserved that it was not recognized as an *Archaeopteryx*. The

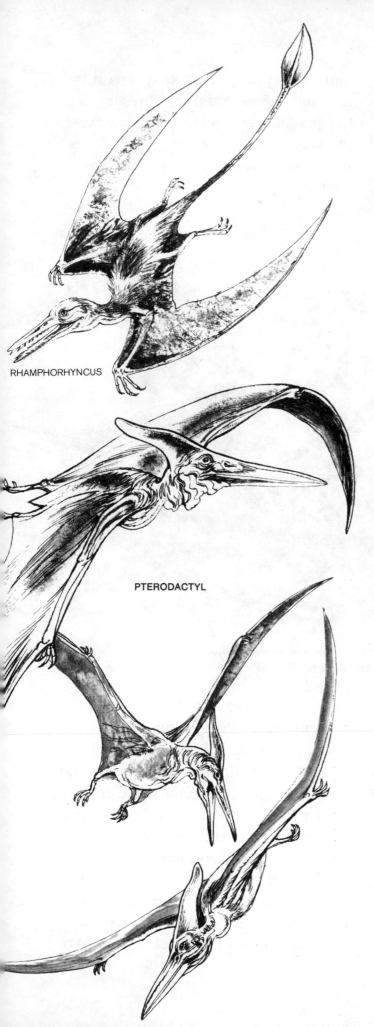

RHAMPHORHYNCUS

PTERODACTYL

owner of the quarry happened to show it to a visiting geologist two years later, who realized that although it was not as good as the first two, it was still extremely important. The owner of the quarry presented the third *Archaeopteryx* to Erlangen University.

In the same quarries at Solnhofen where the *Archaeopteryx* fossils were found, flying reptiles had also been found. These were known as pterosaurs — and most of them were small, ranging from sparrow- to crow-sized. It was not until some time after the discovery of the fossil birds that the huge flying dragon—the pterodactyl—was found in North America. At first many people thought the birds must be descended from the flying reptiles, but Thomas Huxley (a friend of Darwin's) and others correctly believed them to have evolved quite separately.

**Have flying reptiles been found?**

The most significant event connected with the flying reptiles was probably created in 1908 by Herr Wanderer, a German paleontologist, when he decided that the pterosaurs must have been warm-blooded, furry animals. He came to this decision after studying their way of life — if they were scaly and cold-blooded, like other reptiles, they would not be able to fly for hours over the sea. The suggestion seemed outrageous to many scientists. Although it is impossible to prove that they were warm-blooded, since Wanderer suggested that pterosaurs had hair, scientists have found the imprint left by hair

27

in the rocks surrounding fossil ptero-saurs. Many things are still unknown about these giants of the air. Did they lay eggs? If so, did they brood their young, like birds, or leave them, like most other reptiles? Or perhaps they had living young. How long was it be-fore the babies could fly? Presumably, the parents fed them while they were growing. These and many other ques-tions may never be adequately an-swered.

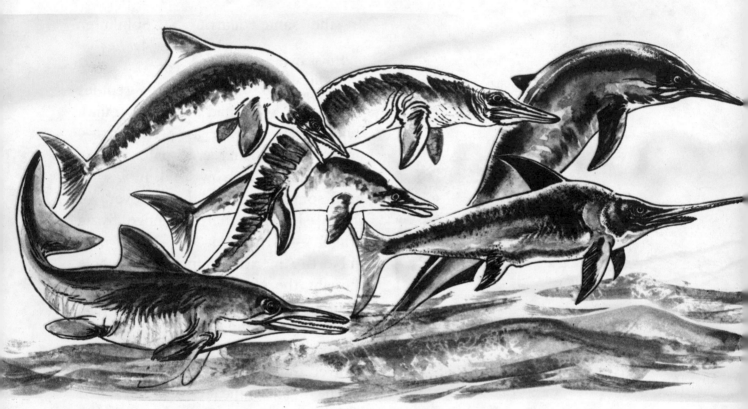

Ichthyosaurs were reptiles that took to the water. In shape they were very similar to certain fish, dolphins, and porpoises.

Many ichthyosaurs (their name means fish-lizards) have been found at Lyme Regis in southern England. Since they lived in and near shallow seas, well-pre-served specimens have often been found and most museums possess well-pre-served ichthyosaurs. Some are partic-ularly interesting — for instance, in Germany, specimens were found in

**Why are ichthyosaurs well-preserved?**

which females were giving birth to their living young. Being completely aquatic and yet air-breathing, like porpoises and dolphins, the ichthyosaurs had to give birth to babies that were fully developed and able to breathe at once. Ichthyo-saurs have also been found in which the remains of their last meal have also been fossilized; and others have been found with pieces of their skin fossilized.

In appearance, some of the ichthyosaurs were very similar to modern dolphins, which are mammals. This is because both ichthyosaurs and dolphins developed from four-legged animals and fed on cuttlefish and other fish. Their feet are used as paddles, the body

Mythical dragons may have been plesiosaurs.

is streamlined, and they have many small teeth, which helps them to hold their slippery food.

The largest ichthyosaur known is *Leptoptergyius,* which had a skull over seven feet long and a total length of more than 36 feet. The ichthyosaurs varied in shape. Apart from the dolphin-shaped

**Which is the largest ichthyosaur?**

ones, there was *Eurhinosaurus,* which looked like a swordfish. Unrelated to the ichthyosaurs were the plesiosaurs. They were also reptiles that had returned to the sea. Like the ichthyosaurs, their legs were changed into paddles, but they had long necks and short tails. There were also short-necked plesiosaurs that had massive skulls. Both groups of plesiosaurs were fearsome predators. One of the largest plesiosaurs was *Elasmosaurus,* which lived during the Cretaceous Period. This was nearly 46 feet long — but a large part of this length was its neck, which contained 76 vertebrae (neck bones). No other animal, living or extinct, is known to possess so many.

Fossil plesiosaurs have been known for hundreds of years — in the past they were often described as dragons. It has been suggested that the type of dragon Siegfried and other notable dragon-slayers fought was based on fossil plesiosaurs — they had long snakelike necks and the front paddles were thought to be wings. When fossils were discovered by chance in quarries, they would have been preserved in the monasteries and palaces as the bones of dragons. This is possibly how the legends about dragons started.

There is really no such thing as a "living fossil." The expression is used, however, to describe animals that are close relatives of animals known from fossils millions of years old.

**What are living fossils?**

Perhaps the most famous of all

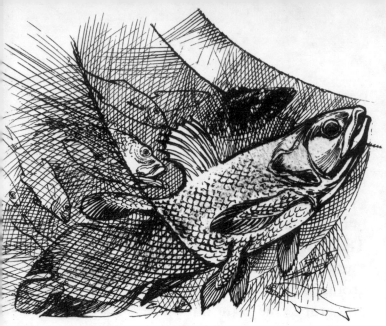

The coelacanth was thought to be completely extinct until one was caught in the Indian Ocean.

pouches, are found only in Australia. Elsewhere, although they were once common, they have become extinct. The duck-billed platypus and the spiny anteater (or echidna) are even more primitive and are the only mammals that lay eggs. They are found only in Australia, New Guinea, and Tasmania.

Nearby is another famous "living fossil," the tuatara, a lizardlike reptile living on islands near New Zealand. It

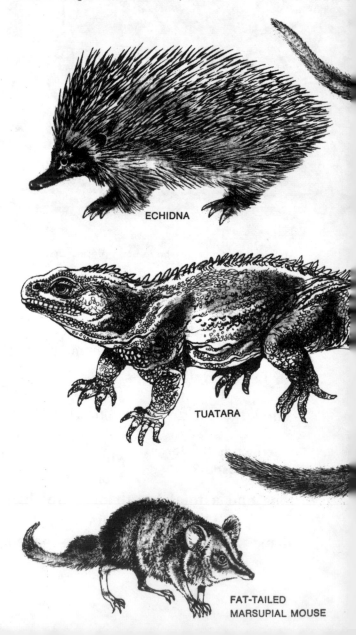

Living fossils. The animals of Australia and New Zealand have been separated from the rest of the world for a long time and are often similar to animals long extinct in other parts of the world.

ECHIDNA

TUATARA

FAT-TAILED MARSUPIAL MOUSE

"living fossils" is the coelacanth, which was once known only from fossils dating from Cretaceous times, and was thought to have been extinct for over 136 million years. Then one was caught by fishermen in the Indian Ocean. The find caused a stir in scientific circles; scientists were able to examine first-hand an animal they thought they would never see alive. Subsequently, several others have been caught from time to time, and some are preserved and can be seen in museums.

Many Australian animals are described

**Why are Australian animals so special?**

as "living fossils." Australia has been cut off from the rest of the world longer than the other parts have been from each other. Many of the animals found there are very primitive and related to species long since extinct in other parts of the world. Apart from a few living in America, marsupials, or mammals with

30

has remained virtually unchanged since its closest relatives walked the earth back in the Jurassic era some 150 million years ago. Similarly, crocodiles have remained more or less unchanged for millions of years.

The ginkgo is a tree that during the Cretaceous Period was found all over the world; today, though, it is found only as a wild tree in eastern China. It can often be seen in parks and gardens.

YAPOK, OR WATER OPOSSUM

PLATYPUS

# The People Who Studied Fossils

Fossils have been found way back into history. In an-

**When were fossils first studied?**

cient times they were thought to be magical, as some primitive people still do. And 2,500 years ago, in the sixth century B.C., ancient Greek scientists discussed fossils and wondered how it was that animals that normally lived at the bottom of the sea were found high and dry in quarries. Famous Greeks like Herodotus and Pausanius decided that the sea must once have covered the land. The Romans, too, were aware that the sea had once covered the land — though they probably merely repeated what the Greeks had discovered.

But after the fall of the Roman Empire, scientific studies of any sort were forgotten in Europe, as first the barbarians conquered Europe and then the Christian Church tried to prevent the study of anything it considered heretic. In particular, experiments were discouraged. Fortunately, the Arabs translated many Greek books. In the period known as the Renaissance, European scientists once and for all broke away from the restrictions of the Church and talked about Greek literature, which had been preserved by the Arabs, and once more started making careful scientific experiments.

31

Leonardo da Vinci, the famous painter,
was also one of
the most inge-
nious scientists
of the Renais-
sance period. Unfortunately, he wrote
most of his notes in code, and as a re-
sult few of his fellow scientists really
knew what he was doing! He was also
a talented engineer, and it was in
order to build canals that Duke Ludo-
vico the Moor summoned Leonardo to
Milan. While supervising the work of
building the canals, Leonardo da Vinci
noticed that numerous shells of sea
creatures were being dug up, and yet
they were miles from the sea. How did
these crabs, mussels, oysters, corals,
etc., get there?

**What discoveries were made during the Renaissance?**

Leonardo da Vinci was aware of
most of the writings of ancient scholars
such as Aristotle and Pliny. Leonardo
agreed with them that these sea creatures were the remains of animals that
had once been alive. His theory was that
the continents where they were found
had been flooded in the past. The shells
and other remains were filled with mud
and gradually turned to stone, or, as in
the case of fish and sea urchins, they
rotted away and fresh mud filled the
space.

Leonardo observed the facts carefully
and from these arrived at his theory,
which was much more logical than most
of the fanciful ideas of the time. In fact,
if one thinks about it carefully, consid-
ering how little was known about fossils, Leonardo was remarkably close to
the truth.

The idea of floods covering the con-

tinents — which had also been suggested several times before Leonardo—
gradually became accepted. One of the
main reasons was that it was compatible
with the Bible. This was very important,
as disbelief in the Bible could often
mean death, torture, or imprisonment
for a scientist. The "deluge" theory en-
abled the study of fossils to make considerable progress — although, in the
end, when it was realized that it was
not in fact the truth, there were bitter
arguments.

A little later, in the middle of the
seventeenth century,
there lived a remark-
able Danish doctor
and naturalist, Neils Stensen. He is usually known by his Latin name of Nico-
laus Steno, as he, like other scientists
at that time, always wrote in Latin and
came to be known by his Latin name.
After studying in Holland and France,
he was invited to the court of Ferdinand
II de Medici in Florence. Florence was
really the center of both the artistic and
the scientific worlds of the time. The
Medici family took special pride in in-
viting outstanding men to court and
supporting their work by giving them
a place to work and money to live on.
Although most of his work was in the
field of anatomy, Neils Stensen took a
particular interest in some fossils that
were to be found in the Medicis' collection in Florence. These were known as
*glossopetrae,* which can be translated
as "tongue-stones." They were just like
pointed tongues made from stone, and
quite common. A few scientists had sug-

**What are glossopetrae?**

Steno dissecting a shark at the court of the Medicis.

gested that they might be sharks' teeth and Neils thought they were probably right. Then he managed to get hold of a corpse of a shark that had been found stranded on the beach and set about comparing the fossil teeth with those of a modern shark. He was soon convinced that (although they were slightly different) the fossil teeth (or glossopetrae) were indeed those of a shark.

Steno also realized that this meant that

**What are strata?**

the extinct sharks lived in a sea that was no longer there. He then set about writing one of the most important books on geology. He pointed out that the layers of the earth, or *strata,* build up gradually and that normally the deepest are the oldest. When they tilt, or go upward, Steno pointed out, the earth had been moved by earthquakes. He noticed that the layers were often distinct and contained different kinds of fossils.

His book was intended as an introduction to an even greater work, but unfortunately for science, Steno then became a priest and discontinued any further scientific work.

The name "Father of English geology"

**Who was the "Father of English geology"?**

is given to William Smith, who was the son of an Oxfordshire blacksmith and was born in 1769. As a schoolboy he was interested in geometry and drawing, and when he left school he was apprenticed to a surveyor. When he was 22 years old, he finished his apprenticeship and started work. His first job was making surveys for coal mines and the routes of canals in north Somerset. He enjoyed his work and spent most of the rest of his life doing the same sort of thing all over England. While he was making his surveys, William Smith became more and more interested in the rocks he saw, and he started to keep careful notes. From them he was able to draw the first geo-

William Smith studying the rock strata.

logical map of England — the various colors of the geological map indicated the types of rocks found.

Another important discovery made by William Smith followed from what Steno had found. William found that different kinds of fossils were often found in the same order within the strata (or layers) of the rocks. He found that some sorts of fossils were always found at the bottom of the rocks while others were at the top, and so on. He also realized that the type of fossil found in a rock was a good way of knowing what kind of rock it was. From all his notes, William was able to draw the first geological column, in which all the rocks are combined into a chart that has the oldest rocks at the bottom and the newest at the top. This was the start of the science called *stratigraphy*. William Smith continued his studies of geology wherever he went until he died in Northampton at the age of 70.

**Who was the most famous woman fossil hunter?**

Over 150 years ago a man named Richard Anning owned a souvenir shop in Lyme Regis. People were just beginning to enjoy bathing in the sea and it was a popular resort. In his shop Richard Anning sold all the usual souvenirs, and also some objects he found along the beach, such as sea urchins, starfishes, shells, and fossils. Richard Anning noticed that the fossils, such as ammonites, were particularly popular, and so he and his daughter Mary collected them along the cliffs around Lyme Regis.

34

Mary Anning collected many fossil reptiles.

Soon Mary was so good at fossil hunting that she often went by herself, and in 1811 she found an ichthyosaur bone. Neither she nor her father knew what it was at the time, but it was put on sale in the shop. Fortunately, it was bought by Sir Everard Home while he was vacationing at Lyme Regis. He was the king's physician and also the professor of anatomy at London University. But even he was not certain what the bone was. After much thought, he published a description of it in 1819 and announced that it came from a giant salamander. Later it was realized that it was a reptile — the ichthyosaur.

Mary continued to find bones, some of which were bought by the British Museum, and by the time she was 21 she was not only a full-time dealer in fossils, but she was quite an expert on them. Having discovered the first ichthyosaur at Lyme Regis, she went on to discover the first plesiosaurs, and in 1828 she found a well-preserved flying reptile.

Gideon Mantell was a country doctor living in Lewes in Sussex. He used to enjoy walking and often walked to see his patients instead of riding a horse; and he would search the embankments and quarries he passed for fossils. He also managed to get his wife interested in some of the strange objects he found on his walks. In 1822 Mrs. Mantell astonished her husband by finding some teeth he was unable to identify. After looking at them carefully, Gideon Mantell decided to send them to a famous anatomist, Baron Cuvier in Paris. Even Cuvier was baffled by the teeth. He identified them as belonging to a rhinoceros.

**Have fossil footprints ever been found?**

Meanwhile, back in England, Gideon had also discovered some enormous footprints in the rock. He did not realize that these footprints were made by the owner of the teeth he had found, but he then found some bones that he felt certain came from the same animal as the teeth. These bones were in Cretaceous strata. Baron Cuvier was still baffled— he thought the new bones might belong to some sort of hippopotamus. Then, more or less together, Baron Cuvier and Gideon Mantell decided that the bones and teeth came from some kind of extinct giant reptile. But it was a long time before the bones were connected with the fossil footprints.

In trying to decide what his extinct reptile looked like in life, Gideon Mantell compared the bones with those of living iguanas. He decided that they were fairly similar. Unfortunately, he was wrong, but the name *Iguanodon* has stuck, and several interesting pictures and models of the mighty animal came into being.

**What did Mantell's reptile look like?**

Mantell wrote a book called *Wonders of Geology,* which became a best seller. He commissioned the famous artist John Martin to illustrate *Iguanodon.* John Martin was well-known for his massive paintings portraying scenes from the Bible — such as the Day of Judgment — and his particular version of *Iguanodon* looked something like a fantastic dragon with an enormous tail and stumpy legs.

When the Great Exhibition (which later became known as the Crystal Palace) opened, Waterhouse Hawkins designed a whole series of models of fossils, including two of *Iguanodon.* These were made from concrete and were life-sized. They still exist today, with many others, on an island in a lake in a park in Sydenham, London. Before the models were finished, a dinner party was held inside the belly of one of the iguanodons, to which Sir Richard Owen and other important scientists of the day were invited.

It was not until half a century later, however, that it was realized that *Iguanodon* was not a clumsy four-footed reptile, but a graceful beast that walked on its hind legs. The "horns,"

35

The dinner party inside the (inaccurate) model of *Iguanodon* at Crystal Palace

An *Iguanodon*

which earlier artists had put on its nose, were actually on its thumbs.

**What is evolution?**

Animals are always changing. Each generation is slightly different from the next. You can see this by looking at your friends, their parents, and grandparents. Although they are often very like their parents, there are always some slight differences. In nature, animals and plants also vary, and some will be better than others at surviving. Those that survive will pass on some characteristics to their offspring, whether it is a seed, an egg, or a baby. The offspring that inherit these characteristics will also be better at surviving. Thus, gradually, the appearance of an animal or plant may change.

**Who was the first to collect evolutionary evidence?**

In 1831, a young man by the name of Charles Robert Darwin had just left Cambridge University. His family hoped he would become a priest, but Charles was really interested only in natural history, and so he was overjoyed when he was offered a chance to go on a trip around the world aboard the H.M.S. *Beagle*. The purpose of the voyage was to make charts, study astronomy, and make various other surveys of natural history, geology and so forth. Charles Darwin was to be the naturalist.

It was from numerous observations that he made on this trip, particularly in the Galápagos Islands, that Charles Darwin eventually developed his theory of evolution. Just as he was about to give a lecture on his ideas, it was realized that another naturalist, Alfred Russel Wallace, who had been in the East Indies, had made exactly the same discoveries about evolution. So they wrote the lecture together, and it was given by Sir Joseph Hooker, the Director of the Kew Botanic Gardens. Although scientists were very interested in the new theory, it did not get very much publicity.

A year later, in 1859, Darwin published a book, *On the Origin of Species by Means of Natural Selection,* in which he explained in more detail how all animals and plants were constantly struggling to survive and that only the fittest could survive.

The book was sold out on the day of publication, but it was still only gradually that the public took an interest in Darwin's theories. Slowly people recognized he was saying that all species

While in the Galápagos Islands, Charles Darwin studied the animals that later led to his theories of evolution.

"evolve," and that they were not a special creation. Although Charles Darwin was a religious man (and nearly became a priest), the scientific world soon became divided and the supporters of Darwin were regarded as irreligious by many. It was to be a long struggle before evolution gained general acceptance. But now zoologists recognize evolution as a fact, although Darwin's original theory has been modified, as more has been learned about subjects such as genetics (the modern science that deals with the little differences in each animal that are passed on to offspring) which Darwin had never even heard of.

Thomas Henry Huxley was a brilliant lecturer, and right from the start he supported Charles Darwin's ideas. Darwin himself did not like to appear in public, as he was rather shy. He liked arguments even less than public appearances, as he was an extremely kind and gentle man. Thomas Huxley, on the other hand, seemed to enjoy a good debate.

**Who was "Darwin's bulldog"?**

In nearly all of the arguments it was Thomas Huxley who spoke out for Darwin — and so became known as "Darwin's Bulldog." Huxley's principal opponent was Bishop Samuel Wilberforce — also a good speaker, and very good at tying his opponents up in knots; in fact, he was so good that he was known as "Soapy Sam." But Soapy Sam was no match for Huxley. Through trying to be too clever at a public debate in Oxford, Soapy Sam said some silly things that allowed Huxley to win an important argument.

Gradually, good sense prevailed — particularly since evolution made it so much easier to explain things like fossils and the changes in the earth's shape — but for those who believed that every word in the Bible was true, it was difficult, if not impossible, to believe.

Edward Cope continued collecting fossils even during the Indian Wars. The Indians regarded him as a friend.

Cope and Marsh. The two names are among the most famous of all American paleontologists, and yet they were

**Who were the most famous fossil collectors in the United States?**

bitter enemies for most of their lives — and even after they were dead!

Edward Cope was born in 1840 and was interested in natural history from an early age. Although his father wanted him to take up farming, Edward eventually persuaded him to allow him to study anatomy. He read Darwin's books, and then at the outbreak of the Civil War he went to Europe to study. By the time he returned to the United States he was a firm believer in Darwin's theory of evolution, and he became a zoology professor at a small college. It looked as if he was going to lead a very quiet life — but then suddenly he gave up his job, sold all his property, and traveled west to look for fossils.

He took seven assistants, some wagons, and a mule train, and set off across Kansas, although the area was full of hostile Indians. His fossil hunting was very successful and soon his home in Philadelphia was overflowing. When his father died, Edward inherited a large fortune. Edward Cope used all his wealth to finance his collecting trips and to buy any other fossils that came on the market. It was while he was in Kansas that Edward Cope first met Othniel Marsh.

Othniel Marsh was the son of a farmer. The family was not particularly well off, but his uncle, George Peabody, became one of the wealthiest men in the country. Uncle George gave considerable money to charity, and also paid for the education of his nephew. He also encouraged Othniel's interest in natural history, and even before Othniel went to the university he had been writing to Louis Agassiz, a famous professor at Harvard University. After Othniel Marsh acquired his degree at Yale, he rapidly rose to be a professor — no doubt helped by George Peabody's generous donations to the university. Marsh

Othniel Marsh and Edward Cope argued constantly and tried to prevent each other from collecting fossils.

became the world's first full-time professor of paleontology, and with Uncle George's money founded what became one of the most important natural history museums in the world — the Peabody Museum in New Haven. Like Edward Cope, Othniel was sent to Europe to study during the Civil War and while he was there he bought numerous fossils which he sent back to the states.

Upon his return, Othniel Marsh set off

**What did the Indians think of fossil collectors?**

on a series of well-organized collecting trips. In the course of these, he became friendly with Chief Red Cloud of the Sioux Indians, and even during the Sioux war of 1876, when General Custer's army was massacred, the Indians still remained friendly with Othniel Marsh and the other scientists who were collecting fossils in South Dakota, Wy-

oming, and Nebraska. Marsh's team was able to collect many fossils. Marsh wanted that exclusive right. When other scientists or collectors tried to start excavations, Marsh would simply offer workmen more money to work for him, and offer a higher price for all specimens. When Edward Cope came along it was a different matter. Although he was not as wealthy as Marsh, Cope could still afford to pay similar prices.

The race was on. Railroad workers,

**What was the "Battle of the Bones"?**

farmers, soldiers, teachers, children — in fact, anyone who could recognize a fossil — made money as Marsh and Cope tried to outbid each other. In next to no time the two men were accusing each other of all sorts of trickery, and Edward Cope even accused Marsh of getting his workmen to smash any fossils they could not carry — just to keep Cope from getting them. Marsh then pored through all the articles written by Cope and published a list of the mistakes Cope had made. Cope replied by claiming that Marsh did not do any of the work himself but used his wealth to pay other people to do the work for him.

The long and bitter quarrel between Othniel Marsh and Edward Cope lasted throughout their lifetime and became known as the "Battle of the Bones." It really got under way in 1877, when a schoolteacher sent Marsh a giant vertebra (backbone) that he had found in Colorado. For some reason, Marsh did not get around to replying, and so when more bones turned up, the schoolteacher sent some to Cope. As soon as Marsh heard that Cope was interested, he bought the entire collection, including the ones Cope had. After other similar events, Marsh thought he had the field to himself, because Edward Cope had run out of money.

Edward Cope became a paleontologist with the U.S. Geological Survey. But in 1879, Marsh was created chief paleontologist and took all the best specimens for the museums where he was curator.

**How did the "Battle of the Bones" end?**

In 1899, Cope tried to prevent Marsh from being reelected president of a geological society. Marsh retaliated by persuading the U.S. Department of the Interior to order Cope to hand over all the fossils to the National Museum in Washington — where Marsh was curator.

This was the last straw! Cope got together with a friend who worked on the *New York Herald* and published a series of sensational articles accusing government departments of corruption and extravagance, saying that under Marsh's influence the best jobs in museums and in the Academy were going to the sons of wealthy businessmen in order to get money from their parents. The outcome was that the U.S. Congress investigated both Cope's and Marsh's claims. Cope was allowed to keep his fossils, but the government also decided that no more public money should be spent on paleontology.

In 1897 Cope died, and by that time Marsh had managed to use up his vast

At National Dinosaur Monument remains of fossil dinosaurs are left partly embedded in rock so that visitors can see how they were found.

Henry Osborn's party discovered nests of fossil dinosaur eggs in Mongolia.

fortune and had become a professor at Yale. Two years later Marsh died, but from beyond the grave Cope "won" the Battle of the Bones when his friend Henry Osborn took over Marsh's old job as chief paleontologist with the Geological Survey.

Henry Osborn went on an expedition

**Where is the National Dinosaur Monument?**

to collect dinosaurs in Colorado which was financed by another wealthy benefactor of museums, Andrew Carnegie. While walking with his assistant, Henry Osborn noticed rocks jutting out of the ground — some of which were as tall as a man. He and his assistant realized suddenly that they were looking at the leg bone of a dinosaur. When excavated, the bone proved to be part of a *Diplodocus,* one of the largest dinosaurs to have walked the earth. A huge part of Colorado and Utah was created a National Park in 1955 and is known as the National Dinosaur Monument. The public can see partly excavated dinosaurs in the ground, just as they were found.

Henry Osborn went on to have a long

**What else did Henry Osborn discover?**

and distinguished career in paleontology. Another of his more famous discoveries was made while he was on an expedition to the Gobi Desert in Mongolia. Dinosaur eggs were found in the desert — even whole nests full. Some of the eggs showed tooth marks where early mammals had tried to open them.

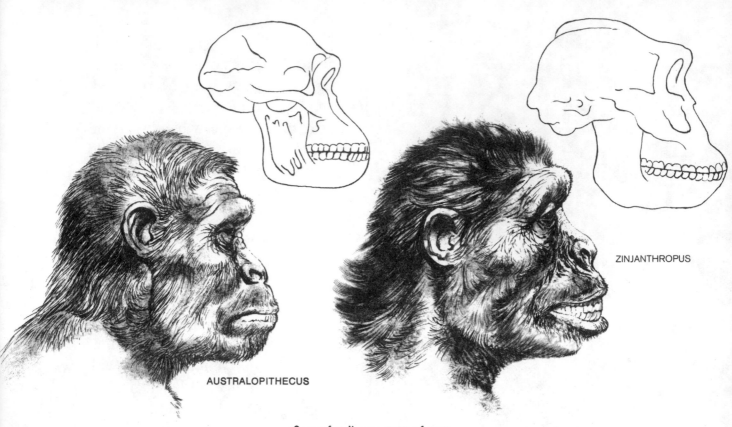

AUSTRALOPITHECUS

ZINJANTHROPUS

Some fossil ancestors of man.

No one knows for sure when man evolved. During the Miocene Epoch some 14 to 24 million years ago was the time when several primitive apes appear to have evolved, including *Ramapithecus,* which may possibly be a direct ancestor of man. The apeman scientists have reconstructed from the fossil remains of *Ramapithecus* looks more apelike than manlike in many ways, but his teeth were similar to those of man. *Australopithecus* (which means *southern* apeman and is *not* connected with Australia) lived about 9 million years after *Ramapithecus.* He was more manlike and walked upright. He may even have used simple tools.

**When did man evolve?**

Then, less than one million years ago, the first "real" men appeared. They were similar to modern men, but had smaller brains. Gradually modern men evolved and eventually the man known as Cro-Magnon man developed and inhabited the world with the ancestors of the humans that now populate it.

Olduvai Gorge in Tanzania is one of the world's most important fossil sites. It is just over 100 miles from Nairobi and is now a favorite spot for tourists in East Africa to visit and see the site where many hundreds of interesting fossils have been found, including several early men. During his lifetime Dr. Louis Leakey and his team of scientists collected hundreds of fossils, including those of early man, apeman, and the animals they hunted. Unlike many other places where

**Where is the Olduvai Gorge?**

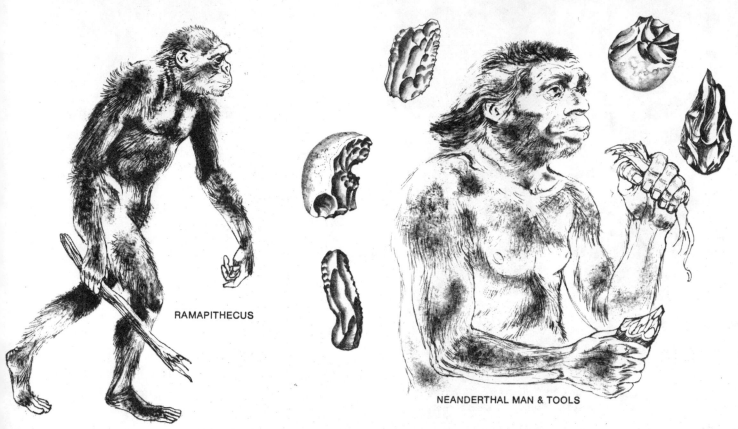

RAMAPITHECUS

NEANDERTHAL MAN & TOOLS

Neanderthal man is shown with some of the flint tools he used.

such fossils have been found, the layers (strata) in which they are found are clearly defined and can be dated accurately. Now visitors can go to the Olduvai Gorge site, where a field museum has been created, and see where the famous fossils were found, and in some cases see fossils and tools still in position. One of the most notable fossils found there is a type of southern apeman *(Australopithecus)*, popularly known as *Zinjanthropus*. A primitive man very closely related to modern man has also been found.

**Who was Neanderthal man?** In 1856, workers in a quarry in the Neander Valley, near Düsseldorf in Germany, found some bones in a crack in the limestone. They were not the least bit

interested in the bones and simply threw them out with the earth. The owner of the quarry was passing by and happened to notice the bones, however. He gathered up as many as he could find and showed the pieces to a local schoolteacher, who realized that they probably belonged to an extinct race of humans. When the schoolteacher, Johann Fuhlrott, announced his discovery at a conference in Bonn in 1857, the other scientists were speechless. An argument started almost immediately, but only a few people believed that Fuhlrott had discovered an extinct human. Most scientists said that the bones came from an old and diseased man. But then two more skeletons similar to those from Neander were found in Belgium. What was more important was that the Belgian bones were mixed up

43

Piltdown man "discovered" in England was later shown to be a forgery.

with those of animals living in the Pleistocene Epoch. This proved beyond all doubt that the fossil men lived long ago. Neanderthal man (as the fossil man first found in Neander has become known) has since been found in many parts of Europe, and scientists have even been able to deduce how he lived.

Piltdown man is one of the most famous

**Why is Piltdown man famous?**

of all fossil men — but he never existed. In 1912 several pieces of skull were found near the village of Piltdown in Kent, not far from London. When they were reconstructed, the skull was found to have belonged to a primitive man with an apelike jaw. As time went on and different fossil men were discovered in other parts of the world, it was realized that the Piltdown man was quite strange and unlike any other fossil men. Then,

in 1953, three British scientists tested the bits of bone, using modern equipment. They found that Piltdown man was made up from the skull of a modern man and an ape's jaw with filed-down teeth! Piltdown man was a fake!

At a small village named Pikermi, close

**Why is the village of Pikermi famous?**

to Athens, Greece, one of the largest collections of fossil mammal bones was discovered. In 1835, a British antique collector discovered a handful of bones while searching for ancient Greek vases and sculptures. A little later, a soldier serving with the troops of Otto Von Wittelsbach (the German who was king of Greece at the time) also found some bones. Among the bones found by the soldier was what he thought was a human skull with diamonds filling the cracks in the bone. Back in Germany this soldier boasted to his friends about his find, and eventually the police found out. He was arrested as a grave robber, but the police were not convinced that the diamonds were genuine and called for expert advice. When scientists looked at the skull, they agreed that the crystals were not diamonds. But they were much more interested in the skull — they realized that it was an ape, not human, and that it dated from the Tertiary Period. This was the oldest known fossil ape.

Soon fossil hunters from all over Europe flocked to Pikermi—which was a good place to spend leisure time in the sun while looking for fossils. They found lots of bones, many of which

Peking men around a campfire with some of the animals they have killed.

were from animals similar to those found in Africa today. The only difficulty was that the bones were mostly mixed up, as they had been washed down a river.

The Stone Age men often hunted fairly large animals, and the remains of these animals have sometimes been preserved around the camps where fossil men lived. Some of the bones were burnt, showing that they had been cooked and eaten by men; other bones were cracked open so that the marrow could be extracted and eaten.

**How do we know what fossil men ate?**

One of the most spectacular discoveries was in Moravia, Czechoslovakia. Here the bones of over one thousand mammoths of various sizes were found. The Stone Age men probably captured them by digging pits across tracks used by the mammoths and covering them over with branches. Hunting large animals, such as rhinoceros, bears, and wild boar, was often dangerous, and some of the bones of Stone Age men are scarred where they have been attacked. But Stone Age men were hardy, and even bad wounds would usually heal.

To the north of Lyons in France is a site where Stone Age man hunted wild horses. There is a cliff over a thousand

45

The ancestors of modern man hunted mammoths. Here they have driven one into a swamp to kill it.

feet high, on top of which is a grassy plain that slopes away in the distance. The Stone Age men drove the horses over the edge, where they fell to the rocks below. Scientists have calculated that as many as 100,000 horses may have been killed here.

In 1879 a little girl named Maria San-

**Were fossil men artistic?** tuola wandered into a passage of the caves at Altamira in northern Spain and suddenly saw enormous paintings of bulls. She told her father, and when he saw these and many other magnificent colored paintings of wild animals, he realized that they were ancient. He thought they had probably been painted by Stone Age men, and reported the discovery to experts, but they did not believe the paintings were very old. It was to be many years before Señor Santuola was indeed proved right: the paintings were the work of Stone Age men.

The most famous cave paintings are those at Lascaux in southwestern France. Unfortunately, the public cannot go in very often, as the air from people breathing and the lights they use makes green algae (microscopic plants) grow on the rocks, and the algae was beginning to spoil the pictures. In order to preserve the paintings, visitors are allowed in the caves only occasionally.

**When were the most recent fossils formed?**

Fossils are constantly being formed. Every single animal or plant that dies could become a fossil but, of course, only a few actually do. Those living in tropical forests are quickly destroyed — ants and other insects soon eat any dread creatures — but those living in swamps, bogs, and similar places may well become fossilized in the same way that other plants and animals did millions of years ago. One of the best places to see fossils in the making is in a peat bog. Peat is the remains of plants. Near the top they are fresh, but ten or twenty feet down the remains of plants are hundreds of years old. Eventually a fossil like coal would form.

Early men painted pictures of the animals they hunted on the walls of caves.

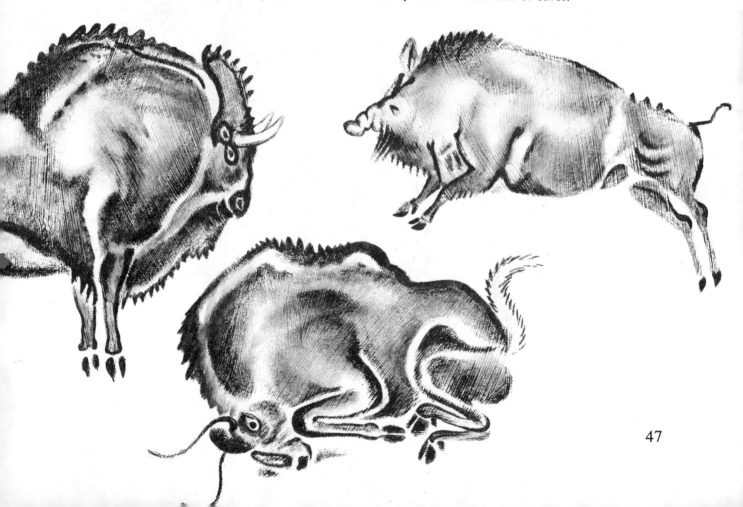

# Index